BRILLIANT WORKING DOGS

Written by Annabel Griffin

Illustrated by Marina Halak

Copyright © 2024 Hungry Tomato Ltd

First published in 2024 by Hungry Tomato Ltd
F15, Old Bakery Studios, Blewetts Wharf, Malpas Road, Truro, Cornwall,
TR1 1QH, UK.

No part of this publication may be reproduced, stored in a retrieval system, or transmitted in any form or by any means, electronic, mechanical, photocopying, recording, or otherwise, without prior written permission of the copyright owner.

A CIP catalogue record for this book is available from the British Library.

ISBN 9781916598751

Printed in China

Discover more at
www.hungrytomato.com

CONTENTS

The World of Dogs	4
Breed Groups	6
Brilliant Working Dogs	8
Sheepdogs and Herders	9
Multipurpose Dog	14
Sled and Cart Dogs	16
Guard Dogs	20
First Responders (Police, Military and Rescue)	22
What's That Dog?	24
Spot the Dog	26
Heroic Dogs	28
Glossary	30
Index	31

Words in **BOLD** can be found in the glossary.

THE WORLD OF DOGS

Get ready to explore the wonderful world of working dogs! From the herding sheepdogs to the guarding great danes, there are so many different types of lovable working dogs to discover.

Wolf or dog? Who knows.

WHERE DO DOGS COME FROM?

Believe it or not, all dogs are **descendants** of ancient wolves. The details of how and when wolves became dogs are still quite foggy, but it likely started when humans began to **domesticate** and train wolves, at least 14,000 years ago. Today, dogs can be found all over the world.

WHAT IS A BREED?

A breed is a particular group of dogs that all share the same (or very similar) appearance and **characteristics**, making them easy to identify. There are hundreds of different breeds, and they can vary wildly in size, shape, hairiness, and personality.

Not all dogs belong to a specific breed. Some dogs, known as mutts or mongrels, are a mixture of lots of different breeds. They can make fantastic pets, and can often be found looking for a loving home at rescue or **rehoming shelters.**

Big and small, they've got it all!

GETTING A DOG?

Maybe you already have a dog in your family, or maybe you'd like to in the future. Owning a dog can be fun and rewarding, but it's also a big responsibility. Some dogs need a lot of space, time and attention. Before buying or **adopting** a dog, you should always carefully research their breed and think about whether you are able to give them everything they need to be happy.

They may be working dogs, but they still love to play!

BREED GROUPS

Dog breeds are often arranged into seven different groups that are loosely based on the jobs that they were originally bred to do.

SPORTING GROUP

Also known as gundogs, these dogs were originally bred to help hunters retrieve birds.

NON-SPORTING GROUP

This is the group for dogs that don't fit into any of the other groups, so they are quite a mixed bunch!

TERRIER GROUP

This group were originally bred to hunt burrowing animals, such as rats, rabbits, foxes, and badgers. Most of them have "terrier" as part of their name.

WORKING GROUP

Dogs in this group were originally bred to perform practical tasks, such as pulling sleds and carts. They were also often used as watchdogs. They are usually large dogs.

SIGHTHOUNDS
These dogs are usually long, lean and very fast.

SCENT HOUNDS
These dogs have droopy ears and powerful noses.

HOUND GROUP

Hounds were bred for their sense of smell or sight, and were usually used for hunting. They can be split into two sub-groups: sighthounds and scent hounds.

HERDING GROUP

This group includes dogs that were bred to work on farms; herding and guarding livestock, such as sheep and cows.

TOY GROUP

Tiny breeds that are small enough to sit in your lap fall into this group. They are bred mostly as pets and companions.

BRILLIANT WORKING DOGS

Dogs and humans have been working side by side for thousands of years. Many breeds of dog have been designed to be good at specific jobs, such as herding, hunting and guarding.

Most working dog breeds have a high level of intelligence, energy and trainability. They can be loyal and loving companions, but often require more time and attention than dogs bred purely for companionship.

SHEEPDOGS AND HERDERS　　9

Border Collie

Bursting with energy and intelligence, border collies are famous for being excellent sheepdogs. They are very loyal and easy to train, but can become bored easily and need a lot of daily exercise.

- Playful people-pleaser
- Athletic body
- Thick coat
- Hard-working

ORIGIN: United Kingdom
COAT: Medium-length, smooth
PERSONALITY: Clever and hard-working

INTELLIGENCE
ENERGY LEVEL 🐾🐾🐾🐾🐾
TRAINABILITY 🐾🐾🐾🐾🐾

10 SHEEPDOGS AND HERDERS

Old English Sheepdog

These giant balls of fluff make great sheepdogs and have even been known to try and herd children! They are friendly, love to explore, and make great walking companions. Their thick coats need a lot of grooming. Some owners actually shave their dog's fur and spin it like wool!

- short furry ears
- There are eyes in there somewhere!
- Super shaggy coat
- Needs a lot of grooming

ORIGIN: United Kingdom
COAT: Long, very thick
PERSONALITY: Gentle and outgoing

INTELLIGENCE: 🐾🐾🐾🐾🐾
ENERGY LEVEL: 🐾🐾🐾🐾🐾
TRAINABILITY: 🐾🐾🐾🐾🐾

Rough Collie

These beautiful dogs were originally bred to herd sheep in Scotland. They are playful, energetic and easy to train. Like the Old English sheepdog, their long, elegant coat needs a lot of grooming.

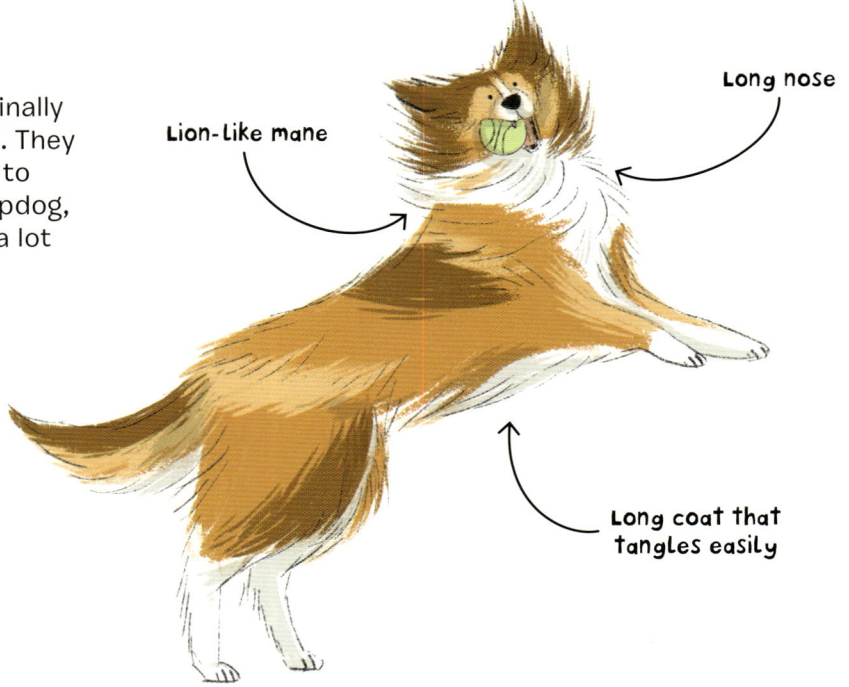

- Long nose
- Lion-like mane
- Long coat that tangles easily

ORIGIN: United Kingdom
COAT: Long, very thick
PERSONALITY: Smart and affectionate

INTELLIGENCE: 🐾🐾🐾🐾🐾
ENERGY LEVEL: 🐾🐾🐾🐾🐾
TRAINABILITY: 🐾🐾🐾🐾🐾

SHEEPDOGS AND HERDERS

Berger Picard (Picardy Sheepdog)

These scruffy French sheepdogs are now a rare breed. They are funny and loyal, and love to play games. They can make excellent companions for active owners.

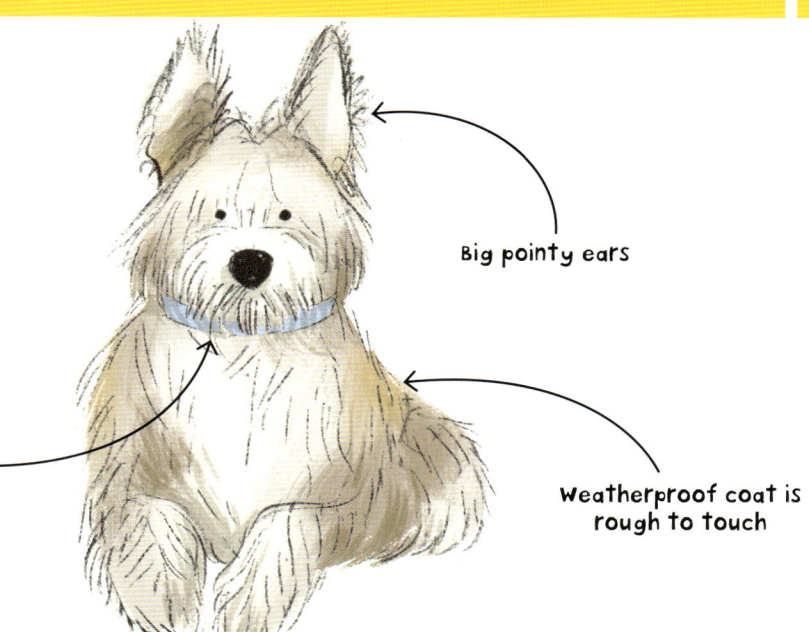

Big pointy ears

Scruffy beard and eyebrows

Weatherproof coat is rough to touch

ORIGIN: France
COAT: Medium-length, **wiry**
PERSONALITY: Playful but sensitive

INTELLIGENCE 🐾🐾🐾🐾🐾
ENERGY LEVEL 🐾🐾🐾🐾
TRAINABILITY 🐾🐾🐾🐾

Australian Shepherd

Despite the name, the Australian shepherd (or "Aussie") was actually first bred in the USA, in the 1800s, to work on the **ranches**. However, they may have been bred from herding dogs brought over to the USA from Australia and New Zealand. They are still often used as a working dog and are popular with cowhands.

Eyes can be brown, blue, amber, or a combination of shades.

Smiley face

Bushy tail

ORIGIN: USA
COAT: Medium-length, thick
PERSONALITY: Active and protective

INTELLIGENCE 🐾🐾🐾🐾🐾
ENERGY LEVEL 🐾🐾🐾🐾🐾
TRAINABILITY 🐾🐾🐾🐾🐾

SHEEPDOGS AND HERDERS

Standard Schnauzer

Schnauzers were originally bred as multipurpose farm dogs, with good skills in guarding livestock and rat-catching. They are very intelligent, alert, and protective, making them good watchdogs.

- Straight back
- Bushy eyebrows
- Bearded snout

ORIGIN: Germany
COAT: Medium-length, wiry
PERSONALITY: Lively and alert

INTELLIGENCE 🐾🐾🐾🐾🐾
ENERGY LEVEL 🐾🐾🐾🐾
TRAINABILITY 🐾🐾🐾🐾🐾

Puli

Is it a dog or is it a mop? This unusual-looking breed was originally used as a herding dog by the **nomadic** Magyar tribes, who settled in what is now Hungary in the 9th century CE. They make great family pets, but their amazing long coats need a lot of looking after.

- Shiny, black nose
- Speedy and acrobatic
- Long, corded coat

ORIGIN: Hungary
COAT: Long, **corded**
PERSONALITY: Fun-loving and friendly

INTELLIGENCE 🐾🐾🐾🐾🐾
ENERGY LEVEL 🐾🐾🐾🐾
TRAINABILITY 🐾🐾🐾🐾

SHEEPDOGS AND HERDERS 13

Pembrokeshire Welsh Corgi

These dogs are famous for being the beloved pets of Queen Elizabeth II of the United Kingdom, but they were originally bred as cattle-herders and guard dogs in Wales. Despite their short legs, they are surprisingly speedy and athletic.

Fox-like face
Big, pointy ears
Long body
Short but powerful legs

ORIGIN: United Kingdom
COAT: Medium-length, thick
PERSONALITY: Loving but independent

INTELLIGENCE 🐾🐾🐾🐾🐾
ENERGY LEVEL 🐾🐾🐾🐾
TRAINABILITY 🐾🐾🐾🐾

Belgian Shepherd

This hard-working breed are more than just great herding dogs. Belgian shepherds are used for a variety of other jobs, including as **service dogs**, guard dogs, police and military dogs.

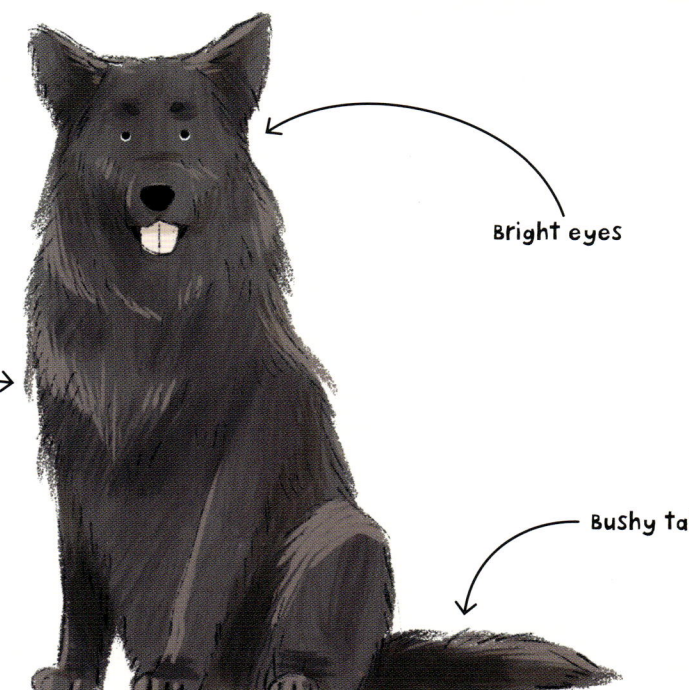

Bright eyes
Shiny coat
Bushy tail

ORIGIN: Belgium
COAT: Long, thick
PERSONALITY: Brave and loyal

INTELLIGENCE 🐾🐾🐾🐾🐾
ENERGY LEVEL 🐾🐾🐾🐾
TRAINABILITY 🐾🐾🐾🐾🐾

14 MULTIPURPOSE DOG

MULTIPURPOSE DOG 15

German Shepherd

One of the most popular working breeds, the German shepherd is a brilliant all-rounder. As the name suggests, they were originally German herding dogs but can tackle just about any job a dog can do. They are often used for police work, search-and-rescue, and are even taken into war zones by the military. They also make good companion and service dogs, and are popular pets.

Pointy ears

Strong legs

Good at agility

ORIGIN: Germany
COAT: Medium-length, thick
PERSONALITY: Confident and brave

INTELLIGENCE 🐾🐾🐾🐾🐾
ENERGY LEVEL 🐾🐾🐾🐾🐾
TRAINABILITY 🐾🐾🐾🐾🐾

SLED AND CART DOGS

Siberian Husky

This well-known dog was first bred by the Chukchi people of Siberia to pull their sleds and for companionship. They are strong dogs, with incredible **endurance** for running long distances in difficult conditions. They are popular pets, but their high-energy, mischievous nature can make them quite a handful.

Loud howler

often have piercing blue eyes

Thick coat to keep warm in freezing conditions

Wolf-like appearance

ORIGIN: Siberia
COAT: Medium-length, very thick
PERSONALITY: Friendly and mischievous

INTELLIGENCE 🐾🐾🐾🐾🐾
ENERGY LEVEL 🐾🐾🐾🐾🐾
TRAINABILITY 🐾🐾🐾🐾🐾

Sled dogs have been used for transport in the Arctic for thousands of years, but these days they are mostly used for leisure and racing events.

SLED AND CART DOGS 17

Samoyed

This stylish fluffy dog is descended from reindeer herders in Siberia. They were originally used for sled pulling, herding, protection and hunting.

Smiley face
Bright white coat is dirt repellent
Fluffy giant

ORIGIN: Siberia
COAT: Long, very thick
PERSONALITY: Gentle and social

INTELLIGENCE
ENERGY LEVEL
TRAINABILITY

Chinook

The Chinook is a rare breed of American sled dog. They were first bred in New Hampshire by the author and explorer Arthur Treadwell Walden, in the early 20th century. The breed was created by **crossbreeding** a Greenland dog (page 18) with a Mastiff/Saint Bernard cross (pages 21 and 23).

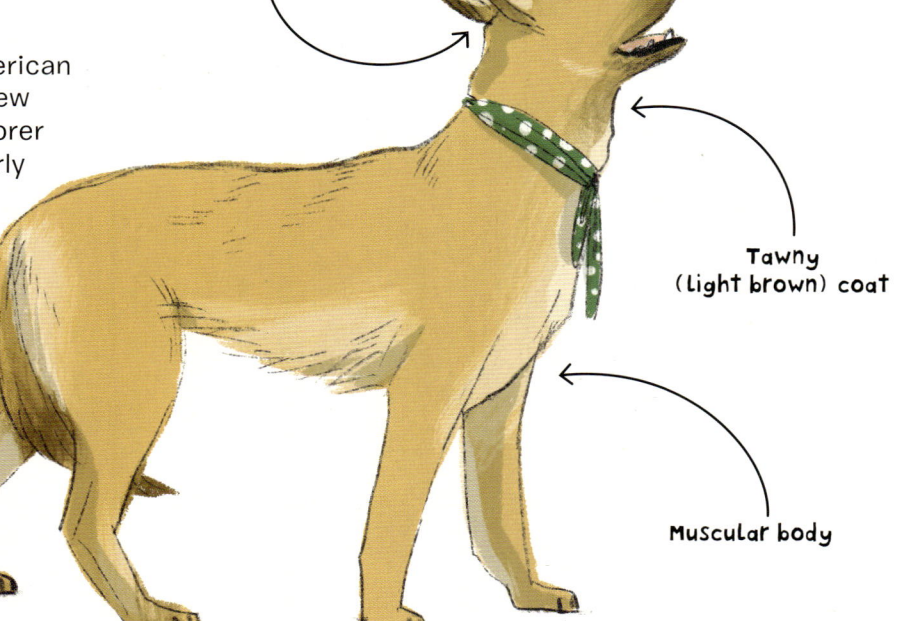

Dark ear tips
Tawny (light brown) coat
Muscular body
Loves children

ORIGIN: USA
COAT: Medium-length, thick
PERSONALITY: Patient and loyal

INTELLIGENCE
ENERGY LEVEL
TRAINABILITY

18 SLED AND CART DOGS

Alaskan Malamute

Although they bear many similarities, the Alaskan malamute is bigger, stronger, and fluffier than their close relative, the Siberian husky (page 16). They are also slower. They were bred to carry heavy loads over long distances.

Feathery tail curls up over its back

Howler

Dense, weatherproof coat

Big paws for digging

ORIGIN: Alaska
COAT: Medium-length, very thick
PERSONALITY: Playful and loving

INTELLIGENCE 🐾🐾🐾🐾🐾
ENERGY LEVEL 🐾🐾🐾🐾🐾
TRAINABILITY 🐾🐾🐾🐾🐾

Greenland Dog

The Greenland Dog is an ancient sled dog breed, which is thought to have changed very little since it was brought to Greenland from Siberia by the Thule people 1,000 years ago. **Genetically,** it is now considered the same breed as the Canadian Eskimo dog.

Wide head

A rare breed of dog

Thick, water-repellent fur

ORIGIN: Greenland
COAT: Medium-length, very thick
PERSONALITY: Loyal and good-natured

INTELLIGENCE 🐾🐾🐾🐾🐾
ENERGY LEVEL 🐾🐾🐾🐾🐾
TRAINABILITY 🐾🐾🐾🐾🐾

SLED AND CART DOGS 19

Bernese Mountain Dog

These dogs were bred to pull carts in the Swiss Alps. They were also used as farm dogs. They are gentle giants who love being outdoors.

- Big, powerful body
- Black and tan markings
- White chest

ORIGIN: Switzerland
COAT: Long, thick
PERSONALITY: Calm and strong

INTELLIGENCE 🐾🐾🐾🐾🐾
ENERGY LEVEL 🐾🐾🐾🐾🐾
TRAINABILITY 🐾🐾🐾🐾🐾

Bouvier des Flandres

This big shaggy dog started out as a farm dog in Flanders, Belgium. It was used for herding and pulling carts. They also make excellent guard and watchdogs.

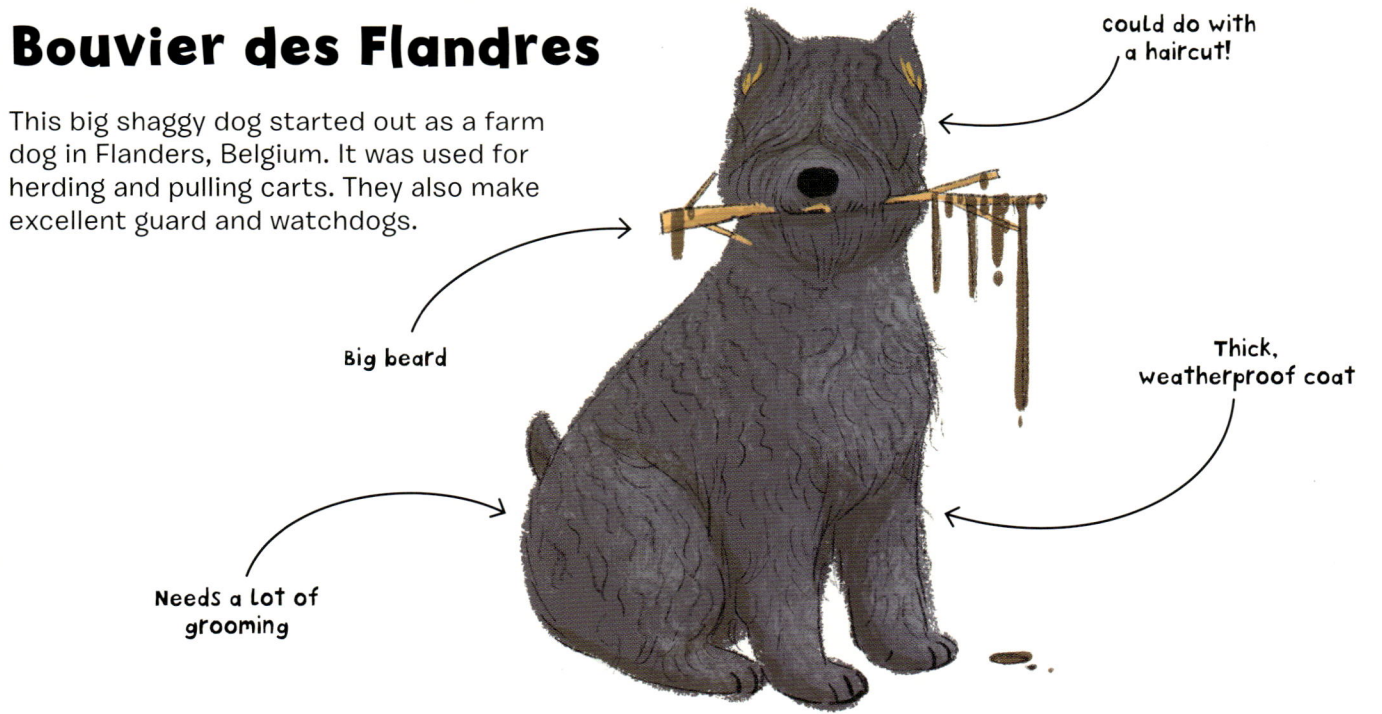

- Could do with a haircut!
- Big beard
- Thick, weatherproof coat
- Needs a lot of grooming

ORIGIN: Belgium
COAT: Medium-length, thick, wavy
PERSONALITY: Fearless and independent

INTELLIGENCE 🐾🐾🐾🐾🐾
ENERGY LEVEL 🐾🐾🐾🐾🐾
TRAINABILITY 🐾🐾🐾🐾🐾

GUARD DOGS

Rottweiler

The size, obedience and fearlessness of Rottweilers makes them excellent guard and security dogs. They may look big and scary, but they can be gentle and loving family pets. They can also have a very playful, silly side.

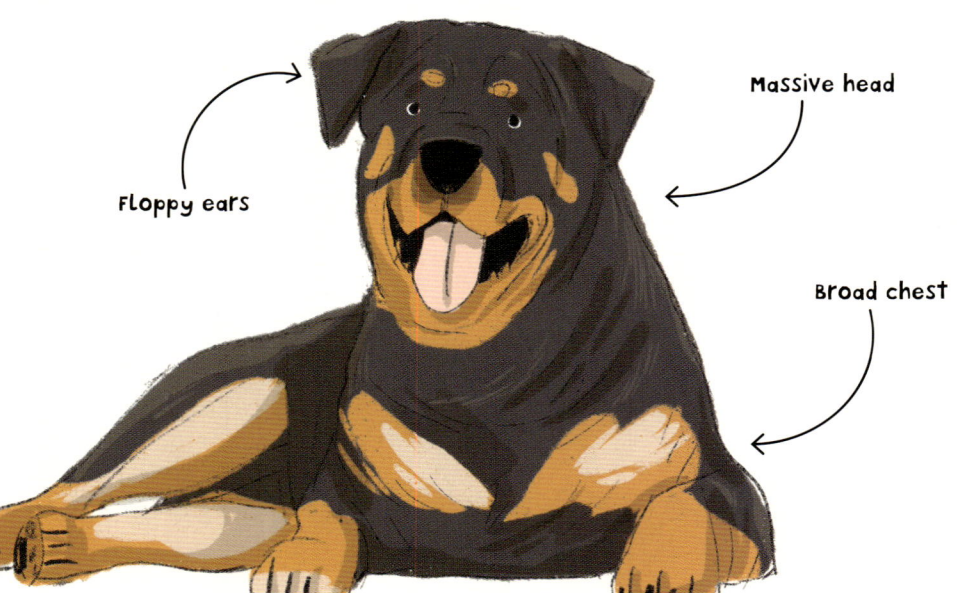

Floppy ears • Massive head • Broad chest

ORIGIN: Germany
COAT: Short, smooth
PERSONALITY: Gentle and obedient

INTELLIGENCE	🐾🐾🐾🐾🐾	
ENERGY LEVEL	🐾🐾🐾	
TRAINABILITY	🐾🐾🐾🐾🐾	

Boxer

Boxers were originally bred as hunting dogs in the 19th century. They are strong, alert and suspicious of strangers, making them great guard dogs. They are very affectionate with their owners.

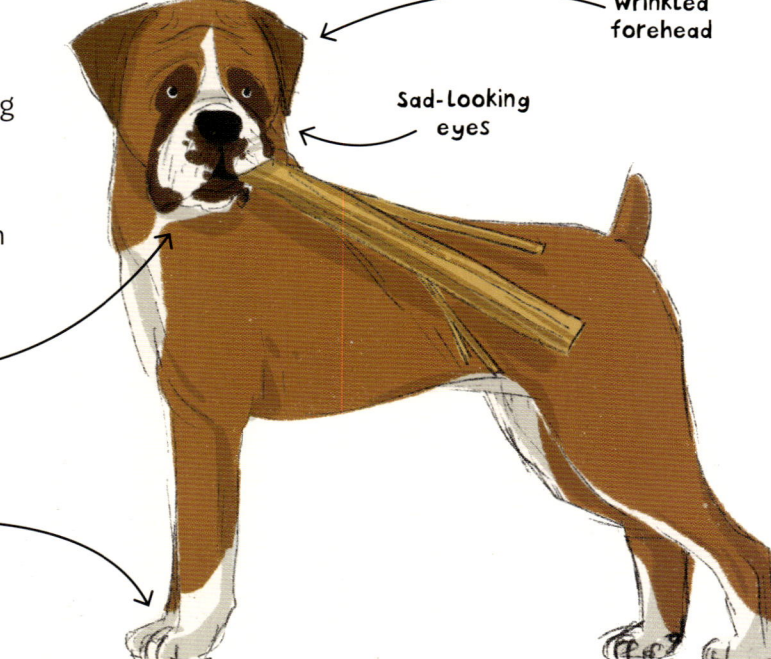

Wrinkled forehead • Sad-looking eyes • Lower jaw sticks out further than upper jaw (**underbite**) • White socks

ORIGIN: Germany
COAT: Short, smooth
PERSONALITY: Fun-loving and alert

INTELLIGENCE	🐾🐾🐾🐾	
ENERGY LEVEL	🐾🐾🐾🐾	
TRAINABILITY	🐾🐾🐾🐾	

GUARD DOGS   21

Great Dane

Great Danes are one of the largest breeds of dog and can measure up to 90cm in height. It's no wonder they make good guard dogs, since their size could scare off any intruder! Don't be fooled; they're really gentle giants.

Long, curved neck

Droopy jowls

Long legs

ORIGIN: Germany
COAT: Short, smooth
PERSONALITY: Friendly and reliable

INTELLIGENCE
ENERGY LEVEL
TRAINABILITY

Mastiff

These mighty dogs have descended from ancient hunting dogs introduced to Britain by the Romans. They have a history of being loyal guardians and protectors. They are very large and weigh between 54 and 104kg.

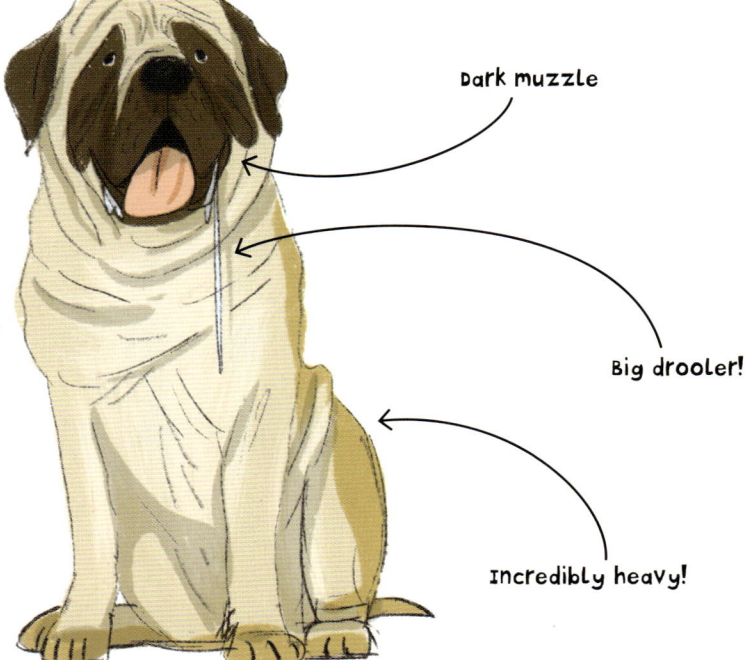

Dark muzzle

Big drooler!

Incredibly heavy!

Strong, chunky body

ORIGIN: United Kingdom
COAT: Short, smooth
PERSONALITY: Protective and loyal

INTELLIGENCE
ENERGY LEVEL
TRAINABILITY

FIRST RESPONDERS (POLICE, MILITARY & RESCUE)

Dobermann (Doberman Pinscher)

This breed have brilliant guarding and tracking skills. They are also speedy and very intelligent. It's no wonder they make good police dogs! They love being part of an active family.

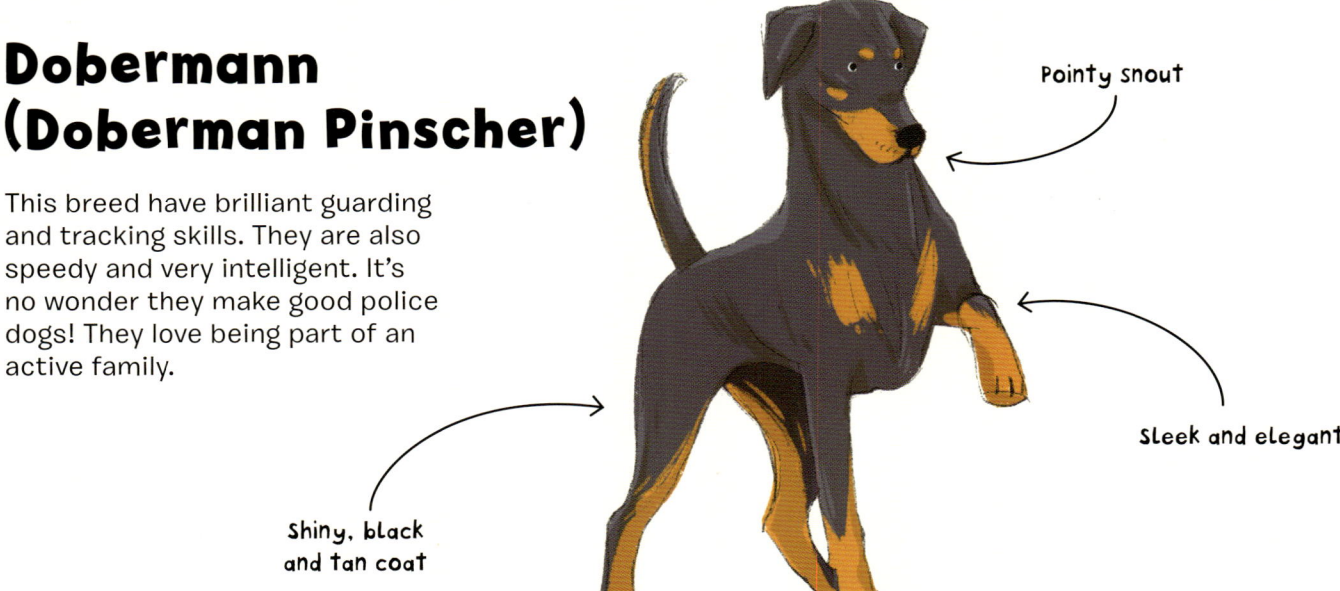

Pointy snout

Sleek and elegant

Shiny, black and tan coat

ORIGIN: Germany
COAT: Short, smooth
PERSONALITY: Alert and fearless

INTELLIGENCE 🐾🐾🐾🐾🐾
ENERGY LEVEL 🐾🐾🐾🐾🐾
TRAINABILITY 🐾🐾🐾🐾🐾

Airedale Terrier

Sometimes called "The King of the Terriers", airedales are the largest of the terrier breeds (see page 6). They were originally bred for hunting, but have a strong history as police and military dogs. In World War I, they were used to carry messages to soldiers behind enemy lines.

Long, flat head

Bearded muzzle

Black saddle markings

ORIGIN: United Kingdom
COAT: Short/medium-length, wiry
PERSONALITY: Sporty and determined

INTELLIGENCE 🐾🐾🐾🐾🐾
ENERGY LEVEL 🐾🐾🐾🐾🐾
TRAINABILITY 🐾🐾🐾🐾🐾

FIRST RESPONDERS (POLICE, MILITARY & RESCUE) — 23

Saint Bernard

This massive dog was originally bred by the monks of the Great Saint Bernard Hospice in the Swiss Alps as guard dogs, but were later used for mountain rescue. They would face difficult and dangerous conditions to rescue people lost in the mountains.

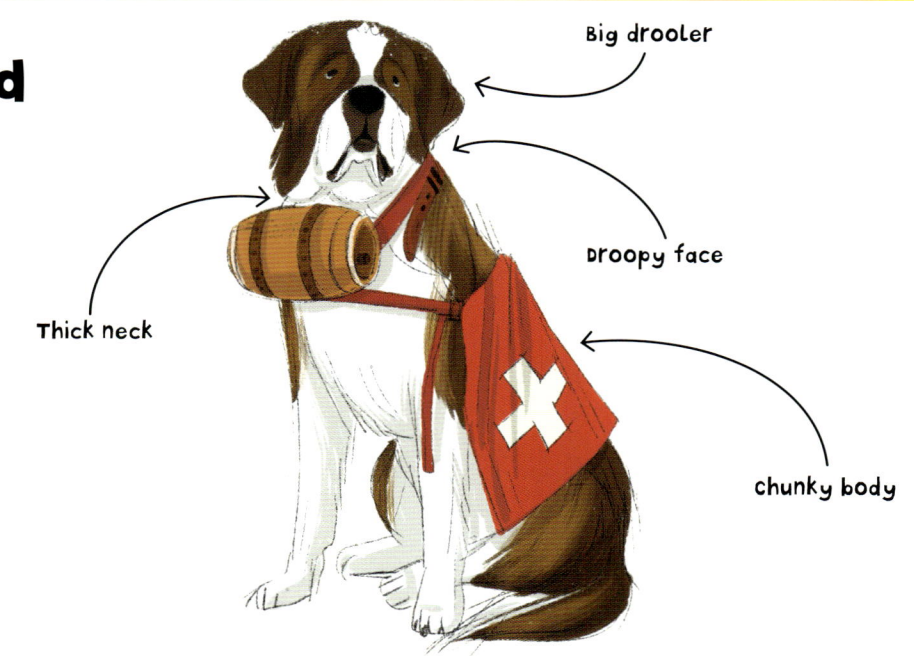

- Big drooler
- Droopy face
- Thick neck
- Chunky body

ORIGIN: Switzerland
COAT: Short, thick
PERSONALITY: Caring and gentle

INTELLIGENCE 🐾🐾🐾
ENERGY LEVEL 🐾🐾🐾
TRAINABILITY 🐾🐾🐾

Newfoundland

These big softies were originally bred as fishermen's dogs, to help retrieve nets. Their strength, courage and swimming skills make them excellent lifesaving, water rescue dogs.

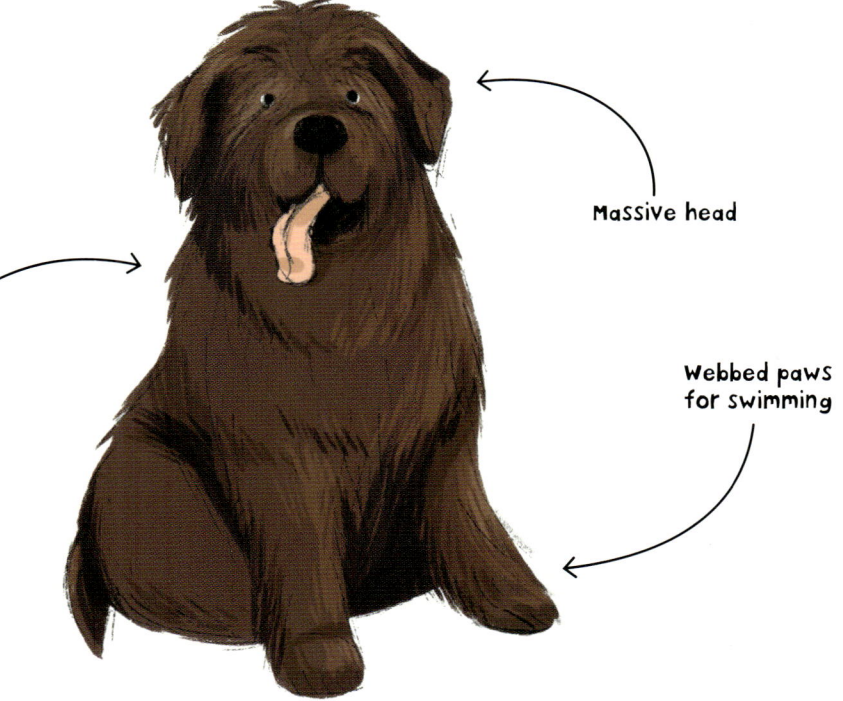

- Massive head
- Webbed paws for swimming
- Thick, water-resistant coat

ORIGIN: Canada
COAT: Long, very thick
PERSONALITY: Sweet and calm

INTELLIGENCE
ENERGY LEVEL
TRAINABILITY

WHAT'S THAT DOG?

Now that you have read all about hard-working dogs, how good are you at identifying them? There are 25 different dogs to figure out. Use the information in the book to help you.

1
What am I?
A. Siberian Husky
B. Greenland Dog
C. Chinook

2
What am I?
A. Saint Bernard
B. Newfoundland
C. Mastiff

3
What am I?
A. Puli
B. Standard Schnauzer
C. Airedale Terrier

4
What am I?
A. Boxer
B. Old English Sheepdog
C. Saint Bernard

5
What am I?
A. Siberian Husky
B. Puli
C. Samoyed

6
What am I?
A. Australian Shepherd
B. Rough Collie
C. Berger Picard

7
What am I?
A. Corgi
B. Standard Schnauzer
C. Puli

8
What am I?
A. Australian Shepherd
B. Old English Sheepdog
C. German Shepherd

9
What am I?
A. Australian Shepherd
B. Border Collie
C. Belgian Shepherd

10
What am I?
A. Samoyed
B. Alaskan Malamute
C. Bernese Mountain Dog

11
What am I?
A. Rough Collie
B. Border Collie
C. Berger Picard

12
What am I?
A. Australian Shepherd
B. Old English Sheepdog
C. Standard Schnauzer

13

What am I?
A. Alaskan Malamute
B. Corgi
C. Great Dane

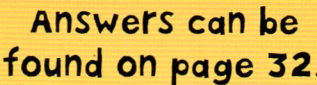
Answers can be found on page 32.

14

What am I?
A. Siberian Husky
B. German Shepherd
C. Chinook

15

What am I?
A. Bouvier Des Flandres
B. Greenland Dog
C. Belgian Shepherd

16

What am I?
A. Corgi
B. Puli
C. Standard Schnauzer

17

What am I?
A. Dobermann
B. Old English Sheepdog
C. Border Collie

18

What am I?
A. Airedale Terrier
B. Dobermann
C. Rottweiler

19

What am I?
A. Boxer
B. Rough Collie
C. Berger Picard

20

What am I?
A. Rottweiler
B. Great Dane
C. Boxer

21

What am I?
A. Chinook
B. Mastiff
C. Alaskan Malamute

22

What am I?
A. German Shepherd
B. Mastiff
C. Samoyed

23

What am I?
A. Dobermann
B. Greenland Dog
C. Husky

24

What am I?
A. Bernese Mountain Dog
B. Newfoundland
C. Mastiff

25

What am I?
A. Chinook
B. Great Dane
C. Bouvier Des Flandres

SPOT THE DOG

There are so many brilliant dogs in the world. You can see them everywhere you go: in towns, parks, and sometimes even at the beach! See which of these are the most popular dogs where you live, make a note of them in a notebook if you do spot them.

German Shepherd   Siberian Husky   Boxer

Airedale Terrier   Rottweiler   Great Dane

Which dogs do you think will be the most and least common in your area? Write your guesses in a notebook and check if you were right. You may be suprised how many you spot, now that you know your breeds!

Border Collie	 **Pembrokeshire Welsh Corgi**	 **Standard Schnauzer**
 **Saint Bernard**	 **Puli**	 **Samoyed**

Have you spotted me when you're out-and-about?

Have you seen me before?

Australian Shepherd	 **Old English Sheepdog**	 **Rough Collie**
 **Mastiff**	 **Dobermann**	 **Newfoundland**

HEROIC DOGS

Man's best friend and man's hero. Take a look at these amazing stories from some of the world's smartest and bravest dogs.

Mountain Rescuer

Barry, a Saint Bernard from Switzerland, saved the lives of more than 40 people. He lived in the Swiss Alps in the 1800s, and rescued people lost in mountain snowstorms. He is still one of the bravest dogs ever! There's even a Saint Bernard Rescue Foundation named after him!

Military Hero

One of the most successful military dogs ever, Lucca, was trained to sniff out explosives. Lucca worked on 400 missions, found 40 explosives, and saved hundreds of lives. She was the first U.S. dog to receive the Dickin Medal for bravery.

I was a mix of German Shepherd and Belgian Shepherd

Firefighter

Eve, a rottweiler from the US, saved her owner Kathie, who was **paralysed** from the waist down, from a burning van. Eve dragged Kathie to safety, saving them both from the fire!

*A lot of dogs have the **instinct** to save their owners' lives.*

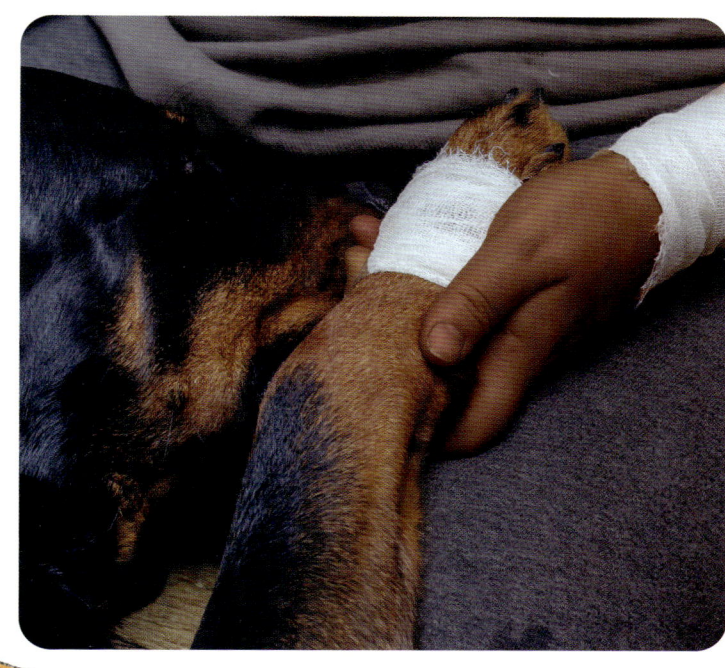

Seaside Lifesavers

Whizz, a Newfoundland from the UK, worked for 10 years as a water rescue dog. In total, he saved 9 people and a dog from drowning! He was given an award for his bravery and lifesaving work.

GLOSSARY

Adopting – Legally taking on the animal as your own, receiving all responsibility.

Agility (dog sport) – a sport where dogs complete complicated obstacle courses, including objects that they have run through, around, under, or jump over.

Characteristics – a feature or quality of a person, place or thing.

Corded – a type of dog coat that forms into long rope-like strands, similar to dreadlocks.

Crossbreeding (crossbreeds) – when two dogs of different breeds have puppies.

Descendants – people or animals that are related to an individual or group who lived in the past. For example, you are a descendant of your parents and grandparents.

Domesticate – to be tamed or trained to live or work with humans.

Endurance – the ability or strength to continue doing something for a long time.

Genetically – how our genes carry information from parents to children.

Instinct – when an animal does something without being trained. They naturally know what to do or how to react to a situation.

Nomadic – nomadic people move around from place to place, with no fixed home.

Paralysed – when someone is unable to move a specific part of their body, usually as a result of illness or injury.

Ranches – large farms for raising horses, cattle or sheep (usually in Mexico, Western United States or Western Canada).

Rehoming shelter – a place where dogs (or other animals) who were lost, stray, or given up by their owners, are looked after until they can be adopted into a new home.

Service dog (or assistance dog) – a dog that has been trained to assist a person with a disability. Examples of service dogs include guide dogs, hearing dogs, medical response dogs, and autism service dogs.

Underbite (or undershot) – when the lower jaw or teeth stick out in front of the upper jaw or teeth, when the mouth is closed.

Wiry – a type of dog coat that is rough, thick and bristly.

INDEX

A
Airedale terrier 22, 26
Alaskan malamute 18
Australian shepherd 11, 27

B
Belgian shepherd 13, 28
berger picard (picardy sheepdog) 11
Bernese mountain dog 19
border collie 9, 27
Bouvier des flandres 19
boxer 20, 26

C
Chinook 17
crossbreed 17, 28, 30

D
Dobermann (doberman pinscher) 22, 27

F
fisherman dog 23

G
German shepherd 14-15, 26, 28
Great Dane 21, 26
Greenland dog 17, 18
guard dogs 12-13, 14-15, 20-21, 22-23

H
herding group 7, 8-9, 10-11, 12-13, 15, 17, 19
hound group 7

M
Mastiff 17, 21, 27

N
Newfoundland 23, 27, 29
non-sporting group 6

O
Old English sheepdog 10, 27

P
Pembrokeshire Welsh corgi 13, 27
police dogs 13, 14-15, 22-23
puli 12, 27

R
rescue dogs 14-15, 23, 28-29
Rottweiler 20, 26, 29
rough collie 10, 27

S
Saint Bernard 17, 23, 27, 29
Samoyed 17, 27
scent hound 7
service dogs 13, 15, 30
Siberian husky 16, 18, 26
sighthound 7
sledding dogs (cart) 16-17, 18-19
sporting group 6
standard schnauzer 12, 27

T
terriers 6, 22, 26
toy group 7

W
working group 6

WHAT'S THAT DOG ANSWERS

1 - B. Greenland dog
2 - B. Newfoundland
3 - C. Airedale Terrier
4 - C. Saint Bernard
5 - A. Siberian Husky
6 - C. Berger Picard
7 - C. Puli
8 - B. Old English Sheepdog
9 - A. Australian Shepherd
10 - A. Samoyed
11 - A. Rough Collie
12 - C. Standard Schnauzer
13 - A. Alaskan Malamute
14 - B. German Shepherd
15 - C. Belgian Shepherd
16 - A. Corgi
17 - C. Border Collie
18 - C. Rottweiler
19 - A. Boxer
20 - B. Great Dane
21 - A. Chinook
22 - B. Mastiff
23 - A. Dobermann
24 - A. Bernese Mountain dog
25 - C. Bouvier Des Flandres

ABOUT THE AUTHOR

Annabel is a writer and artist based in London, UK. Having worked as a bookseller for many years, she now writes children's books focusing on animals and the natural world. Her recent titles include *What Can I See in the Wild?*, *Seasons* and *The Spectacular Lives of Sharks*.

ABOUT THE ILLUSTRATOR

Marina is a talented illustrator of children's books from Ukraine. Her stunning illustrations are inspired by her own childhood, children, nature, magical moments and fairytales.

Picture Credits:
(abbreviations: t=top, b=bottom, m=middle, l=left, r=right)

ANURAKE SINGTO-ON 28bl; Anastasia Vetkovskaya 25tr; Calipson88 26tl; Chris Christophersen 24tl; Christian Kohlhausen 24bl, 27ml; David Pegzlz 25mr; Dimitriev Mikhail 29tr; DiLi Don 25t; Earl Wilkersen 26mr; EKATERINA SOLODILOVA 25ml; Elayne massaini 27tl; EmiliaGraceH 25br; Everydoghasastory 27tr; Eve photography 24br; Fred12 24tl; Gabor Kormany 26tr; Icemanphotos 25ml; Igor Plotnikov 25mr; Ingrid Pakats 29bl; Julia Kuznetsova 28tl; Katechris 26tm; Kateryna Orlova 24ml; Larstuchel 25ml; Marco Germadnik 24mr; muroPhotographer 27m; Otsphoto 26ml; Pchela Vladimir 27tm; PROMAI 24ml; Ricatimages 25bl; Rita_Kochmarjova 27mr, 27tl; SasaStock 25bm, 27bm; Schelmanova Natalia 25tl; Serova_Ekaterina 26m; Sofia Dudova 24bm, 27tr; TMart 24ml; Verky01 24tm, 24mr, 27br, 27tm; Waldemar Dabrowski 25bl, 27bl; Xkunclova 25tr; Yuliya Shatskih 25bm.

Every effort has been made to trace the copyright holders, and we apologise in advance for any unintentional omissions. We would be pleased to insert the appropriate acknowledgements in any subsequent edition of this publication.